W9-CED-419

Revised Edition

Peyton Manning

By Jeff Savage

AMAZING ATHLETES

Lerner Publications Company • Minneapolis

Copyright © 2013 by Jeff Savage

All rights reserved. International copyright secured. No part of this book may be reproduced, stored in a retrieval system, or transmitted in any form or by any means—electronic, mechanical, photocopying, recording, or otherwise—without the prior written permission of Lerner Publishing Group, Inc., except for the inclusion of brief quotations in an acknowledged review.

Lerner Publications Company
A division of Lerner Publishing Group, Inc.
241 First Avenue North
Minneapolis, MN 55401 U.S.A.

Website address: www.lernerbooks.com

Library of Congress Cataloging-in-Publication Data

Savage, Jeff, 1961–
    Peyton Manning / by Jeff Savage. — 2nd rev. ed.
        p.   cm.
    Includes index.
    ISBN 978-1-4677-0874-6 (lib. bdg. : alk. paper)
    1. Manning, Peyton—Juvenile literature. 2. Football players—United States—Biography—Juvenile literature. I. Title.
    GV939.M289S27 2013
    796.332092—dc23 [B]   012015179

Manufactured in the United States of America
1 – BP – 7/15/12

TABLE OF CONTENTS

Peyton Manning *(right)* shakes hands with John Elway *(left)* after joining the Denver Broncos in 2012.

ON THE MOVE

On March 20, 2012, National Football League (NFL) **quarterback** Peyton Manning stood under the bright lights. But he wasn't playing in a football game. Peyton was at a **press conference**. He was there to announce his plan to play for the Denver Broncos. Peyton had been a member of the Indianapolis Colts for 14 seasons. But he was moving on.

Peyton is one of the most successful quarterbacks to ever play in the NFL. He was named NFL Most Valuable Player (MVP) four times with the Colts. No other player has been named MVP more than three times.

Peyton throws a pass while playing for the Colts in 2007.

In 2007, Peyton and the Colts beat the Chicago Bears in the Super Bowl. Peyton threw for 247 yards and a **touchdown**. He was named MVP of the game. But Peyton doesn't like to brag. He knows that football is a team sport. "It was a wonderful team game," Peyton said after the 2007 Super Bowl. "Everyone did their job."

Indianapolis was the only NFL team that Peyton had ever played for. But a neck injury caused him to miss all the 2011 season.

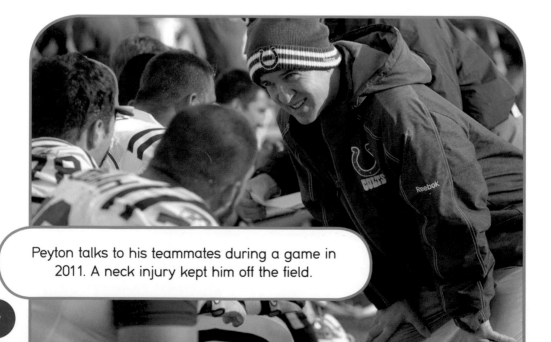

Peyton talks to his teammates during a game in 2011. A neck injury kept him off the field.

New Colts quarterback Andrew Luck talks to reporters.

The Colts weren't sure if Peyton would be able to return to football after his injury. The team decided to **draft** a new quarterback named Andrew Luck.

Peyton's neck injury healed, and he began throwing the football again. The Broncos had a hot young quarterback named Tim Tebow. But the team decided to take a chance on Peyton.

Quarterback Tim Tebow carries the ball while playing for the Broncos.

He signed a **contract** with Denver. The team would pay the quarterback $96 million over five years. Peyton had already earned millions of dollars in the NFL. His new contract made him one of the highest-paid players ever.

The Broncos traded Tebow to the New York Jets. Swapping Tebow for Peyton was a risky move for the Broncos. Peyton is 36 years old. Most NFL players are much younger. Tebow is just 24 years old. He is also very popular with Broncos fans. But Broncos vice president

John Elway knew that quarterbacks as good as Peyton don't come around very often. "I don't consider it much of a risk, knowing Peyton Manning," Elway said.

Peyton knows there is a lot of pressure on him to help the Broncos win right away. The team is paying him a lot of money. Peyton probably only has a few more years to play football. "We're going to do whatever we can to win right now," Peyton said at his press conference. "That's all I'm thinking about."

Broncos fans cheer on their team.

Peyton's parents—Archie Manning and Olivia Williams—both went to the University of Mississippi. The school is nicknamed Ole Miss.

BORN TO THROW

Peyton Williams Manning was born March 24, 1976, to Archie and Olivia Manning. Olivia had been the homecoming queen at the University of Mississippi, where Archie had also been a star player. Archie had been an NFL quarter-back for 14 years, playing mostly for the New Orleans Saints.

Peyton and his brothers—Cooper and Eli—lived with their parents in New Orleans, Louisiana. They often watched their father play.

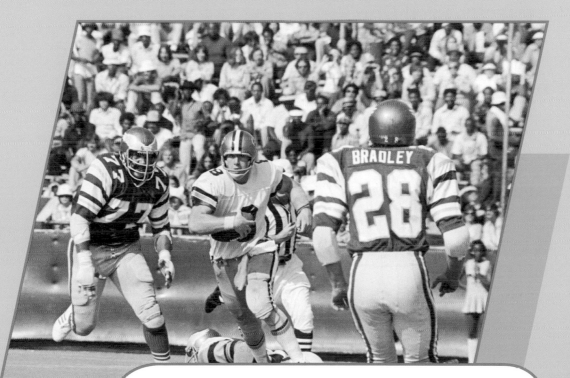

Archie *(running with ball)* played for the New Orleans Saints for 12 years. Even though Archie played well, the team wasn't very good during his career.

Peyton loved football from the start. By the age of three, he was playing the game with his father and older brother Cooper in the living room. Archie would carry a tiny football and try to scoot past his boys on his knees. By the age of four, Peyton was throwing his little football perfectly. Each Christmas, Peyton and his brothers would find gifts of helmets, jerseys, and other football gear beneath their tree. Peyton dreamed of someday being a quarterback, just like his dad.

Peyton went to Isidore Newman School from kindergarten through high school and earned good grades. In 1991, he became the quarterback for the school's **varsity** team.

Cooper Manning got a serious disease just before he started college. He was to play football for Ole Miss. The surgery he had to have ended his football career.

Peyton had dreamed of being at Ole Miss with his brother Cooper. When that dream came apart, he decided to start fresh at the University of Tennessee.

Cooper was his favorite **wide receiver**. Before Peyton got the ball, he'd make secret hand signals to his brother. Cooper knew exactly where to run, and Peyton would throw him the ball.

Peyton played quarterback for the varsity for three years. During that time, he led Isidore Newman to 35 wins and just five losses. Many colleges wanted Peyton to play football for their teams. He picked the University of Tennessee in Knoxville.

Peyton deeply respects his father *(right)*. In college, he wanted to match Archie's success at Ole Miss.

STUDENT OF THE GAME

Peyton was proud to wear the orange-and-white uniform of the Tennessee Volunteers. In 1994, as a freshman, he was the **third-string** quarterback. Even though he didn't play yet, he practiced hard. He wanted to be ready to play if the team needed him. Peyton was needed sooner than anyone expected.

In the first game of the season, the first-string, or starting, quarterback got hurt. Two weeks later, the second-string quarterback got hurt too. Suddenly, Peyton was the team's quarterback.

Peyton was named the starting quarterback in his first year at the University of Tennessee.

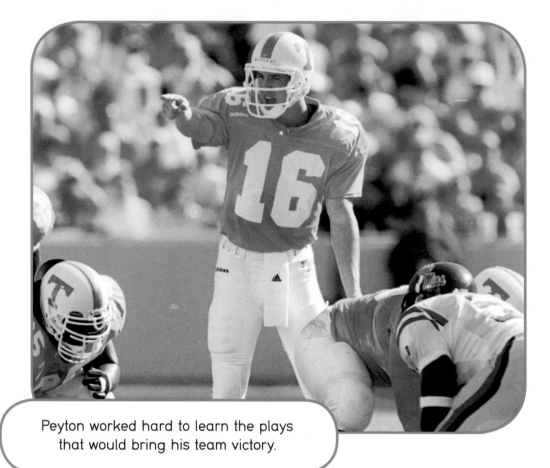

Peyton worked hard to learn the plays that would bring his team victory.

In his first game, he was careful not to throw an **interception**. The Volunteers won, 10–9. Peyton grew more confident. He led his team to six wins in its last seven games. He even guided the Volunteers to a 45–23 win over Virginia Tech in the Gator Bowl.

Peyton was a serious college student who earned good grades. He also studied the football team's **playbook** and looked at **game films**. Peyton's hard work paid off. In the 1995 season, he set team records for **completions** and yards passing. The University of Tennessee was named one of the best teams in the country.

Tennessee head coach Phillip Fulmer *(left)* worked with Peyton throughout his time at the University of Tennessee.

By 1996, Peyton had become a statewide hero. When people saw him at restaurants or malls, they chanted his name. The town of Knoxville, Tennessee, named a street Peyton Manning Pass. Peyton was uncomfortable with all the fuss. In 1997, his senior season, he led the Volunteers to an 11–1 record. They earned the right to play in the Orange Bowl.

College bowl games take place after the regular season is over. They show off the country's best teams.

Peyton holds up the jersey of the Indianapolis Colts, the team that drafted him in 1998.

ALL-PRO THROWER

Peyton knew he wanted to play in the NFL after he finished college in 1998. Many football experts thought he was sure to be one of the first players chosen in the 1998 NFL Draft. The Indianapolis Colts had the first pick, and they chose Peyton.

The Colts offered Peyton a contract for $48 million to play for them for six years. Peyton agreed and immediately set up the PeyBack Foundation. This group gives money to people in need.

But Peyton had a big job ahead. The Colts were losers. They had won just three of 16 games in the 1997 season. Most **rookie** quarterbacks don't play in their first year, but the Colts really needed Peyton's help.

Peyton's first season was tough. Here, he's getting tackled by a member of the New York Jets.

At training camp, before the start of his second season, Peyton ran sprints to become faster and more fit.

He struggled, winning just three games in the 1998 season. "It was frustrating," Peyton said. "But you can either sit there and feel sorry for yourself or learn from it and do something about it."

Peyton worked harder than ever to get himself ready for the 1999 season. He lifted weights and ran sprints. He memorized the team playbook—not just the plays for the quarterback but every play in the book. Could he help his team be a winner?

Peyton studied hard to learn the Colts' playbook. Soon his coaches trusted him to change plays on the field.

Peyton focused on playing well in the 1999 season. He turned the Colts into winners. Indianapolis's 13–3 record was the biggest improvement in NFL history. Six of the wins were fourth-quarter **comebacks**, showing that

Peyton was calm in the final minutes. The Colts even made it to the NFL **playoffs** but lost the first playoff game.

Peyton married his college girlfriend Ashley Thompson in 2001.

The Colts won 10 games in the 2000 season to reach the playoffs again. Unfortunately, they lost again. The Colts had a worse season in 2001, with six wins and 10 losses. In the 2002 season, Peyton's team reached the postseason yet again. This time, the Colts lost to the New York Jets. Indianapolis went to the playoffs in 2003, 2004, and 2005. Each time they lost and failed to reach the Super Bowl. Indianapolis put all of these playoff losses behind them after the 2006 season. The Colts were Super Bowl champions, and Peyton was the MVP of the game.

Peyton and his brother Eli *(right)* with their father, Archie *(center)*.

NEW TEAM LEADER

Peyton Manning is one of the most successful and highest-paid players in the NFL. But the money and fame haven't lessened his interest in giving back to the community. The PeyBack Foundation gives hundreds of thousands of dollars every year to Toys for Tots and Boys & Girls Clubs of America.

In August 2005, Hurricane Katrina almost

destroyed Peyton's hometown of New Orleans. Many people lost their lives. Homes and businesses were ruined across the city and state.

Peyton and his younger brother, Eli, quarterback of the NFL's New York Giants, decided to do something. They helped the American Red Cross load an airplane with supplies. They even flew to Baton Rouge, Louisiana, to help unload the supplies. They also visited shelters where people who had lost their homes in the storm were staying.

Many parts of New Orleans were damaged by Hurricane Katrina.

After finally winning the Super Bowl at the end of the 2006 season, Peyton was on top of the world. A few days after the game, he appeared on the *Late Show with David Letterman*. A few weeks later, he hosted *Saturday Night Live*.

Peyton didn't celebrate for long. His focus soon turned back to football. The Colts played well in 2007 and 2008. But they were knocked out of the playoffs by the San Diego Chargers both years.

Indianapolis only lost two games during the 2009 season. Then they took down the Baltimore

San Diego quarterback Philip Rivers *(left)* shakes Peyton's hand after a playoff game.

Peyton throws a pass against the New Orleans Saints during the Super Bowl.

Ravens and the New York Jets in the playoffs. The Colts were headed to the Super Bowl for the second time in four years! They would face the New Orleans Saints.

Peyton was excited to take on his hometown team in the big game. His teammates and coaches knew they could count on their star quarterback. "When he goes up against the best, he takes his game to another level," said former Indianapolis coach Jim Caldwell. As expected, Peyton played well. But New Orleans won the game, 31–17.

Peyton played in all 16 games of the 2010 season and led his team to a record of 10–6. The Colts lost to the Jets in the first round of the playoffs. Soon after, Peyton said there was a problem with his neck. He had several surgeries and was forced to sit out the entire 2011 season. When his neck was healthy again, Peyton joined the Broncos.

Peyton is excited to get a fresh start in a new city. Can he lead his new team to the Super Bowl? With Peyton Manning throwing the ball, the sky is the limit for the Broncos.

Peyton *(right)* worked hard to recover from his injury.

Selected Career Highlights

2012   Agreed to play for the Denver Broncos

2011   Missed entire season with neck injury

2010   Finished second in the NFL in passing yards (4,700) and touchdowns (33)

2009   Named NFL MVP for the fourth time

2008   Named NFL MVP for the third time

2007   Named Super Bowl MVP
Named Walter Payton NFL Man of the Year

2006   Led all quarterbacks with 31 touchdown passes

2005   Led all players in votes for 2006 Pro Bowl
Named Walter Payton NFL Man of the Year

2004   Named NFL MVP for the second time
Set the record for most touchdown passes in a single season

2003   Named NFL co-MVP
Set NFL record for throwing at least 25 touchdown passes in six straight seasons
Selected to Pro Bowl for the fourth time

2002   Selected to Pro Bowl for the third time

2001   Led the American Football Conference (AFC) in passing yards

2000   Broke team record for touchdown passes in a season, with 33
Selected to Pro Bowl for the second time

1999   Selected to Pro Bowl for the first time

1998   Selected first in the NFL draft

1997   Finished his college career with 33 school records and two NCAA records

1996   Became first Tennessee quarterback to pass for more than 3,000 yards in a season

1995   Selected Associated Press third team All-America

1994   Named Southeastern Conference Freshman of the Year

Glossary

comebacks: wins in the final minutes of games after a team has been losing

completions: catches of passes from the quarterback

contract: a written deal signed by a player and his or her team. The player agrees to play for the team for a stated number of years. The team agrees to pay the player a stated amount of money.

draft: a yearly event in which all professional teams in a sport are given the chance to pick new players from a selected group

game films: videotapes of games that players and coaches can study

interception: a pass that is caught by a person on the defense. An interception results in the opposing team getting control of the ball.

playbook: a book that describes plays a team will use in games

playoffs: a series of games played after the regular season has ended

press conference: an interview held for news reporters

quarterback: in football, the person who throws or hands off the ball

rookie: a player who is playing his or her first season

third-string: the name given to the third player at a certain position. The first-string player is the starting player. The second-string player replaces the first-string player and so on.

touchdown: a score in which the team with the ball crosses its opponent's goal line. A touchdown is worth six points.

varsity: the school team made up of the most experienced or best players

wide receiver: a player who catches passes, mainly for a big gain

Further Reading & Websites

Kennedy, Mike, and Mark Stewart. *Touchdown: The Power and Precision of Football's Perfect Play*. Minneapolis: Millbrook Press, 2010.

Savage, Jeff. *Eli Manning*. Minneapolis: Lerner Publications Company, 2013.

Savage, Jeff. *Tim Tebow*. Minneapolis: Lerner Publications Company, 2013.

Official NFL Site
http://www.nfl.com
The official National Football League website that provides fans with game action, biographies of players, and information about football.

Peyton's Website
http://www.peytonmanning.com
Peyton's official website, featuring trivia, photos, and information about Peyton and his PeyBack Foundation.

Sports Illustrated Kids
http://www.sikids.com
The *Sports Illustrated Kids* website covers all sports, including football.

Index

Photo Acknowledgments

The images in this book are used with the permission of: Rick Wilking/Reuters/Newscom, p. 4; © Andy Lyons/Getty Images, pp. 5, 27; Doug Kapustin/MCT/Newscom, p. 6; AP Photo/Michael Conroy, p. 7; © Jeff Gross/Getty Images, p. 8; AP Photo/Jack Dempsey, p. 9; © University of Mississippi, p. 10; © Bettmann/CORBIS, p. 11; © Scott Halleran/Allsport/Getty Images, p. 13; © Jamie Squire/Getty Images, p. 14; © Jonathan Daniel/Allsport/Getty Images, p. 15; AP Photo/Mark Humphrey, p. 16; © Reuters/CORBIS, p. 17; © Jamie Squire/Allsport/Getty Images, p. 19; © Al Bello/Getty Images, p. 20; © Brent Smith/Reuters/CORBIS, pp. 21, 22; © Sporting News/Icon SMI, p. 24; Marty Bahamonde/FEMA, p. 25; AP Photo/Denis Poroy, p. 26; AP Photo/Denver Broncos, Eric Bakke, p. 28; Brian Ach /AP Images for DIRECTV, p. 29.

Front cover: Rick Wilking/REUTERS/Newscom.

Main body text set in Caecilia LT Std 55 Roman 16/28.
Typeface provided by Adobe Systems.